lea

guitar

... a handy beginner's guide!

Published by **Wise Publications**

Exclusive Distributors: Music Sales Limited,
14-15 Berners Street, London W1T 3LJ, UK

Order No. AM1008414
ISBN 978-1-78305-456-5

Edited by Ruth Power.
Inside layout by Fresh Lemon.

Made in China.

www.musicsales.com

Introduction

This flipbook will get you playing the guitar in no time!

You'll learn the basic techniques you need, the essential chords and how to strum.

Let's get started!

Contents

Know your guitar

- headstock
- tuning pegs
- fretboard
- soundhole
- nut
- bridge
- frets

Getting Started

In the next section we'll look at posture, but for now try to find a chair that's not too low, definitely not an armchair or couch, so you can just about place your feet on the floor.

You'll also need a tuner and a spare set of strings just in case.

Holding the guitar

Sit with your feet flat on the floor, or upright on a stool, and perch a bit at the front of the seat. The guitar should rest on your right thigh, and hopefully you'll find it more-or-less balances there with just a little help from your left hand, which lightly grips the neck.

The front of the guitar should face away from you so you can't see it if you look down.

Hand positions

Whether standing or sitting, the left-hand position is important. The thumb should stay behind the neck, positioned at about the 2nd fret, and the hand should form a gentle curve so that the fingers can come down onto the fretboard at right angles.

This way, you can be sure that the fingertips are making contact with just the strings they need to touch, and not getting in the way of any of the others.

Holding the neck

The right hand, whether strumming or picking, should hang loosely over the front of the guitar at the sound hole (if your guitar is acoustic) or the pickups (if it's an electric).

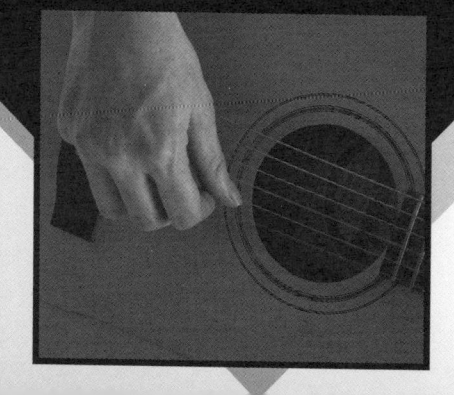

Holding the pick

The flatpick, or plectrum can be used instead of the fingers for a crisper, brighter sound.

Hold the pick between your right thumb and index finger—exert a fair amount of pressure without straining. As you can see, only a small part of the pick should project beyond the edges of your thumb and finger. Your wrist should stay relaxed.

Feel with your fingers

As you start to learn new chords, strumming techniques or anything else involving your hands, there will be a great temptation to look down at your hands to make sure they're in the right place.

But, since you shouldn't be able to see the front of the guitar if you're holding it right, you'd need to hunch right over or twist the guitar up towards you before you can see what you're doing. So get used to feeling for the right position with your fingers.

Try sitting with a mirror in front of you to avoid craning your neck to see your fingers.

GUITAR LEGENDS

Jimi Hendrix

Widely considered as one of the most influential rock guitarists of all time, **Jimi Hendrix's** style involved heavy distortion and the use of amplifier feedback which was previously deemed undesirable. Hendrix also helped to popularise the wah-wah pedal and stereophonic phasing in rock music. Those who witnessed Hendrix' live show would be struck by his magnetism and natural playing style, with his use of effects and signature licks seeming effortless.

He blended single-note runs with chords seamlessly and used chord voicings that even accomplished guitarists would struggle with. For many, Jimi Hendrix challenged what rock music could sound like.

Essential tracks:
'Hey Joe'
'Purple Haze'
'Foxy Lady'
'Star-Spangled Banner'

Tuning

Getting the guitar in tune is a crucial skill. There are various methods which all involve adjusting the pitch of the open strings by turning the tuning pegs to tighten or loosen each string until it sounds the correct note.

You can tune against a piano or a tuning fork; or else you can use an electronic tuner, which will tell you when your guitar is in tune. Either way, start with the thickest (bottom) string, and work your way through the strings to the thinnest (top).

These diagrams show the desired notes on the piano, the equivalent musical notation and the appropriate strings on the guitar.

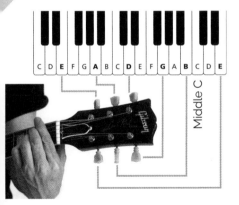

Relative tuning

If you tune the bottom string accurately, you can then use that string to tune the others. Here's how it works:

- Place a finger on the 5th fret of the bottom (sixth) string—this will give you the note you need (A) to tune the open fifth string.
- Once that's done, play a note on the 5th fret of the fifth string. It'll be D, which is the note you need for the open fourth string.
- And again, play a note on the 5th fret of the fourth string to give you the note you need (G) for the open third string.

- Now the sequence changes: this time, play a note on the 4th fret of the third string to sound B, which is the correct note for the open second string.
- Finally, play a note on the 5th fret of the second string to sound E, which is the note you'll need to tune the top string. Check the following diagram for fret positions for each of the reference notes.

Electronic tuners

Using an electronic tuner has lots of advantages: they're pretty fool-proof, and very precise.

Play the bottom string, and the device will show you on its display whether you're low or high.

Tune the string in the right direction and, when it's up to pitch, the display will let you know.

Simply move on to the next string and so on, until the instrument is tuned.

This tuner attaches to the headstock.

GUITAR LEGENDS

Chuck Berry

Chuck Berry helped to shape rhythm and blues. His clean guitar sound and economical playing influenced blues bands such as The Beatles and The Rolling Stones and many more. His style was to mix Chicago Blues with a swing feel that made it more accessible, defining the sound of rock 'n' roll.

It was not only his sound but his performance that had a great influence on subsequent rock music. Berry was flamboyant on stage utilizing guitar solos and showmanship learned from T-Bone Walker to create a spectacle to be seen not just heard.

Essential tracks:
'Johnny B. Goode'
'Maybellene'
'Roll Over Beethoven'

Chords

The first thing you'll learn to play on the guitar are chords, which are groups of notes strummed together. Chords are written down using chord diagrams, or chord boxes.

Here's how they look:
The thicker line at the top is the **nut**.

The horizontal lines are **frets**.

The vertical lines are the **strings**, and the dark dots show where fingers are placed on the strings.

If an X appears above a string, this string shouldn't be played, and with an O, the string is played 'open': without any fingers on it.

Chord Diagrams

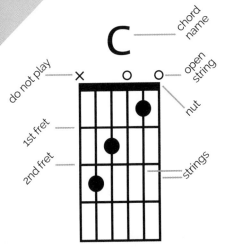

chord name

do not play

open string

nut

1st fret

2nd fret

strings

C

Your first chords

To start playing songs, you only need to know two chords, so let's start with A and E. Try placing the 1st finger on the 2nd fret of the fourth string: Then, add the 2nd and 3rd fingers on the third and second strings, also on the 2nd fret (see below).

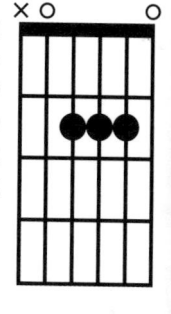

A

Press the strings down as near as you can to the fret without them actually being on the fret. If you're pressing very hard to get a clear sound, there might be something a bit wrong with your finger position, so stop again and check that.

If you brush down lightly across the strings with your right thumb, you'll hear the result. You may find that some of the notes are a bit muffled, so see if you can adjust the fingers until each note sounds out clearly.

E chord

The second chord is E major. E is a great chord for bringing out the full character of your guitar. It uses all six strings, and it looks like this:

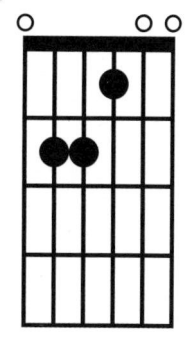

Make a note of the position of the 2nd and 3rd fingers relative to each other. They're next door to one another, just as they were for the A chord.

For now your right hand can simply curl up slightly and strum down across the strings. We'll get into some more advanced strumming soon.

Chord changes

You'll notice, playing chords on the guitar is easy enough: the challenge is often changing from one chord to another.

Finding any similarities you can between chord shapes will give you a head start, and that's just what we're going to do now.

Take a look at the next exercise: it's four 'bars' long, and alternates between the A and E chords. Play the exercise slowly through, and try to keep a steady beat.

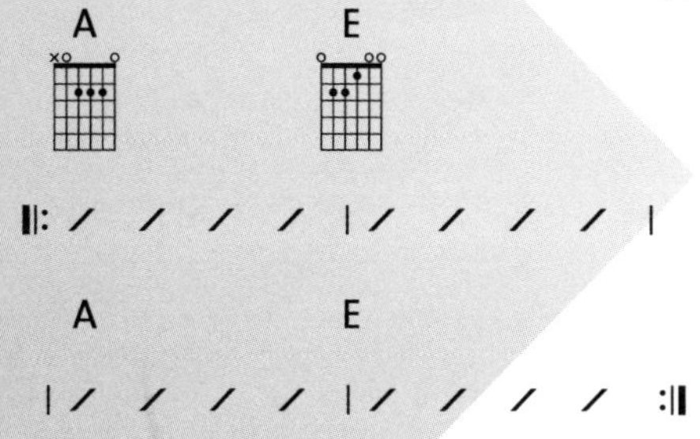

A   E

‖: ∕ ∕ ∕ ∕ | ∕ ∕ ∕ ∕ |

A   E

| ∕ ∕ ∕ ∕ | ∕ ∕ ∕ ∕ :‖

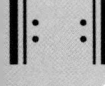

These are repeat marks, and are found either side of a repeated section of music. In this case, they indicate simply that the whole of the music should be played again.

Strum down each time you see a slash (╱). Each slash represents a single beat of music. Four strums of A will make a bar, and then it's time to play a bar of E.

The first few times, you might prefer to strum once on A, and count the four beats out while you change to E. Try to play the E chord right at the beginning of the new bar.

Count again and change back to A, and so on. Once you have done it several times, you'll be able to strum slowly through, once on each beat without having to pause to change the shapes.

GUITAR LEGENDS

Robert Johnson

Robert Johnson was one of the most formative blues musicians that ever lived, though none of his commercial success was seen in his lifetime. There are many stories surrounding Johnson and how he came to play the guitar so well, some say that he made a deal with the devil where in exchange for his soul he received unrivalled guitar skills.

Among the first and most influential of the Delta bluesmen, Johnson recorded just 29 songs in his short 27 years, but his songs introduced themes that form the basis of modern blues and blues based genres today.

Essential tracks:
'Dust My Broom'
'Sweet Home Chicago'
'Ramblin' On My Mind'
'Crossroads'
'Love In Vain'

Quarter notes

Up till now we've used simple rhythm slashes to show the count, but in standard rhythm notation a stem is added to the note head to show that the note lasts for a beat.

This note value is called a quarter note (also known as a crotchet in the UK). The stem can point up or down, depending which is tidiest in the music.

stem————   ————note head

In strumming patterns where rhythm slashes are used, a stem is sometimes also added:

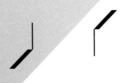

Knowing the quarter-note will help you to read chord charts and tablature. You'll learn more note values throughout this flipbook which will enable you to read basic music rhythms.

Starting to pick

Picking is an essential part of guitar technique, especially in acoustic styles such as country and folk, and it's widely used in blues, ragtime and some types of jazz too, so it's worth spending some time on it.

In this next exercise, the thumb is going to pick just the bottom string of the chord on the first beat, and again on the third beat. The lowest note of a chord is called the bass note. Now, the bass note of the A chord is on the fifth string, but on the E chord it's the sixth string.

Alternate the picked bass notes with strummed chords by brushing the strings down with the backs of the fingernails.

On beats 2 and 4, strum the whole chord as before. Try this exercise, slowly and steadily at first:

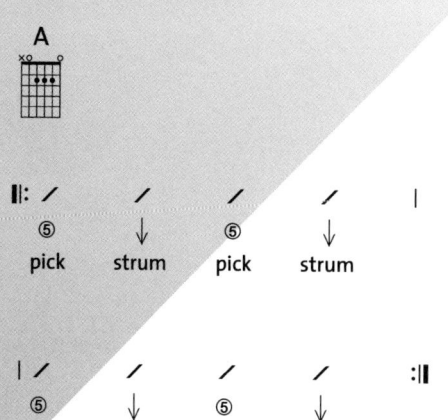

With this next exercise, pick and strum the A chord as before, but alternate with the thumb between the fifth string and the sixth string. It'll create a rhythmic bass line in a country style reminiscent of the music of Johnny Cash.

A

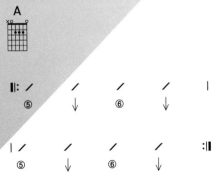

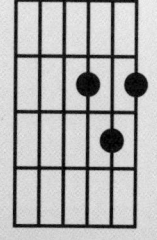

D

Finally, let's try another chord shape. This one goes well with A and E. It's the chord of D. It only uses four strings, so take care when strumming not to play the bottom two strings by mistake.

D

E^7

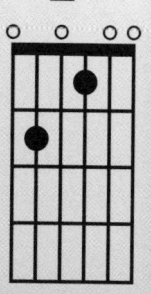

This new chord is a variation of the E shape.

You can play it by taking a finger away from the E shape:

E⁷

GUITAR LEGENDS

Eric Clapton

Through his involvement in many successful bands (Yardbirds, Cream, Blind Faith, Derek and the Dominos) and prolific solo work, **Eric Clapton** has continually redefined his own blues guitar style.

His style is adventurous and impassioned but at the same time careful and precise. His influence includes introducing to the style of blues; feedback, sustain and perhaps most importantly, volume.

Clapton has been inducted into the Rock and Roll Hall of Fame three times and remains one of the most legendary guitarists alive.

Essential tracks:

'Layla' (Derek and the Dominos)

'Bell Bottom Blues' (Derek and the Dominos)

'Crossroads' (Cream)

'White Room' (Cream)

More chords

Here are some more chords for you to become familiar with.

The new shape of G needs special care. You might find it easist to put the little finger into position first, then move the 2nd and 3rd fingers into place.

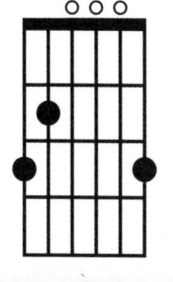

G

G

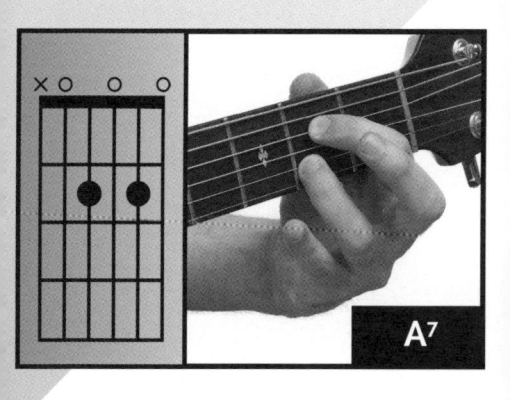

A⁷

Checkpoint

So far you have learned:

- how to hold and tune the guitar
- the main chords within the A, and D major keys.
- how to read chord diagrams
- how to change chords
- how to strum and pick basic patterns

Make sure you have mastered these topics before you move on to learn more chords, including minor chords and how to read tablature.

More chords

Here are some more major chords and dominant 7th chords to add to your growing chord bank.

C

For F, place the 1st finger across the 1st fret of both the first and second strings. This is known as a barre.

F

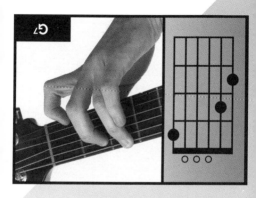

G7

D⁷

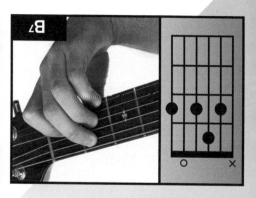

B7

Minor chords

Minor chords have a different sound, but are often used in combination with the ones we've already covered. Minor chords are indicated by the letter 'm' after the chord name as shown below.

Am

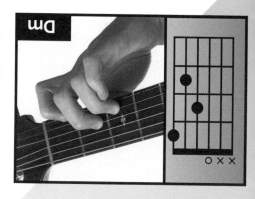

Dm

O X X

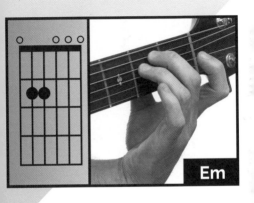

Em

Jimmy Page

Not only is **Jimmy Page** one of the greatest riff-makers and shredders of all time, he is also well respected as a songwriter and producer. With a staggering back-catalogue of great songs and solos the guitarist of Led Zeppelin has well and truly earned his place in rock history.

Page is admired for his excellent taste with his playing, having impeccable timing and a good ear for the right solo at just the right time. He carefully crafted his guitar tone and style to transcend the typical stereotypes of the guitar and used a full range of dynamic control to punctuate his sound.

Essential tracks:
'Dazed and Confused'
'Heartbreaker'
'Kashmir'

Reading tablature

For strumming chords, diagrams showing left-hand finger positions are sufficient.

But when it comes to finger picking, guitarists use a more complete notation system. This is tablature, or tab.

Tablature is a musical notation system for stringed instruments that shows the performer exactly where to play each note on the fretboard.

The tablature system consists of six horizontal lines, each representing a guitar string. The bass string is the bottom line of the tablature staff, and the treble string is the top line.

This layout is inverted from the actual string positions on the instrument. Here, the high-pitched notes lie high on the staff and the low-pitched notes lie low on the staff.

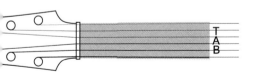

A number on a line indicates at which fret to depress that string. This example describes all six strings of an E^7 shape, picked in turn, starting with the lowest.

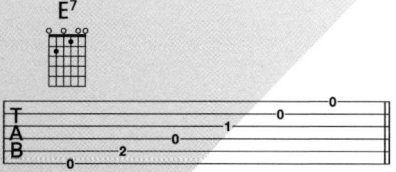

Sometimes, the stems and beams above or below the staff denote the rhythm. In this example, the rhythm is a series of eighth notes.

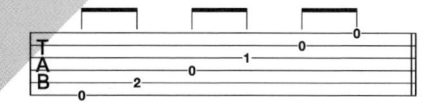

Eighth notes

The eighth note (also called a **quaver** in the UK), is so named as there are 8 of these note values in a basic bar. Where two eighths are played within one beat they are joined by a beam.

For some strumming and tab rhythms the slashes or numbers now have tails and are joined in pairs indicating that each strum is worth half a beat. Two eighth notes make a quarter note.

Where two or more notes are played simultaneously, they are stacked up on the stave.

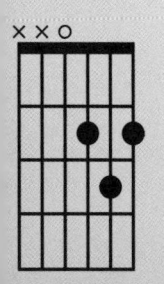

Compare these diagrams with the equivalent notes shown in tab to see how this works.

```
      0
T     1
      2
A     2
B     0
```

Finger picking

To start with, you strummed all the notes of the chord at once. Then, we added picked bass notes. Now we'll play the notes of the chord individually to create finger picking patterns.

Your thumb is the pivot point of all finger picking. Let's build up a pattern little by little on an E chord. Eventually the pattern will require your right thumb, together with the 1st, 2nd and 3rd fingers. The fingers will remain on the top three strings throughout, with the thumb moving to whichever string is needed for the correct bass note.

Try the following exercise, be sure to use the correct finger each time. Start by slowly moving your thumb back and forth from the sixth string to the fifth string.

Give two beats to each bass note: Add a note on the second string played at the same time as the bass notes—use your 2nd finger for these second-string notes: Next, add notes in between on the top string, with the 3rd finger: Try adding a note on the third string, played with the 1st finger.

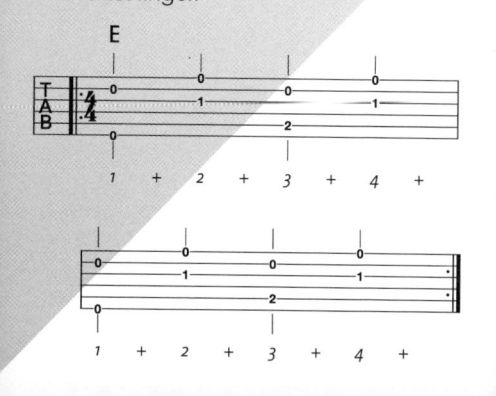

The next exercise shows notes of two chords played one after the other. This type of pattern is known as an arpeggio. Compare the chord diagrams with the notation, and pick the passage slowly through until the arpeggios are smooth.

Am

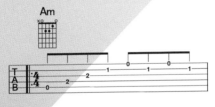

D⁷

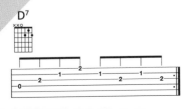

STEVIE RAY VAUGHAN

Despite a musical career that lasted only seven years, **Stevie Ray Vaughan** is one of the most influential blues guitar players in history and is largely responsible for the revival of blues in the 1980s.

His signature sound was with clean amplifiers and high volume with a passion for vintage music equipment.

He chose to use a minimal amount of effects pedals in favour of combining several amplifiers together to create his tone.

With an almost overwhelming passion for the blues, Vaughan's big, bold, bright playing still inspires many guitar players today.

Essential tracks:
'Love Struck Baby'
'Cold Shot'
'Look At Little Sister'

What you've learnt:

- the essential major, minor and 7th chords
- how to read chord diagrams and tablature
- how to strum and pick basic patterns

Now it's time to find some of your favourite songs to learn to play! Look for guitar tab music or lead-sheets with chord boxes to learn from. You might like to use the **Music Flipbook Guitar Chords** as a reference for any chords you may find unfamiliar.

Keep learning

To learn more about playing the guitar and add
more songs to your repertoire, try these titles:

- **The Complete Guitar Player** AM977328
- **The Beatles Guitar Songbook** NO18491
- **Legendary Acoustic Guitar Songs** AM1003310

Recommended listening

Now that you've got to grips with the fundamentals of guitar playing, try listening to how the professionals do it!

The songs listed below all feature classic guitar parts; some are more difficult than others, but armed with the basic techniques you've learnt in this flipbook, you should soon be able to approach some of them.

'Don't Look Back In Anger' (Oasis)
'Everybody Hurts' (R.E.M.)
'Everything Must Go' (Manic Street Preachers)
'Hey Joe' (Jimi Hendrix)
'How Soon Is Now?' (The Smiths)
'Jumping Jack Flash' (The Rolling Stones)
'Parklife' (Blur)
'Smells Like Teen Spirit' (Nirvana)
'Tears In Heaven' (Eric Clapton)
'Waterfall' (The Stone Roses)
'Wild Thing' (The Troggs)
'Won't Get Fooled Again' (The Who)
'Yesterday' (The Beatles)